I0804170

Bobcat and Rabbit

by Jillian Walker
illustrated by Viviana Garofoli

Practice Decodable 28

Mc Graw Hill Education

Bothell, WA • Chicago, IL • Columbus, OH • New York, NY

MHEonline.com

Copyright © 2015 McGraw-Hill Education

All rights reserved. No part of this publication may be reproduced or distributed in any form or by any means, or stored in a database or retrieval system, without the prior written consent of McGraw-Hill Education, including, but not limited to, network storage or transmission, or broadcast for distance learning.

Send all inquiries to:
McGraw-Hill Education
8787 Orion Place
Columbus, OH 43240

ISBN: 978-0-02-145641-3
MHID: 0-02-145641-0

Printed in China

8 9 10 11 12 DSS 27 26 25 24 23

Bobcat sits still and naps on logs.

Bobcat is fast. He has plans.

Rabbit stands in grass.

Bobcat hops up! He runs fast.

Is Rabbit as fast as Bobcat?

Rabbit zigs and zags. He is fast!